MW00980294

THE ADVENTURES OF SEEK & SAVE

THE VILLAGE

PRESENTED TO

_____

BY

_____

LUKE 19:10
"JESUS SAID: "THE SON OF MAN HAS COME
TO SEEK AND SAVE THAT WHICH IS LOST"

THE ADVENTURES OF
SEEK & SAVE

THE VILLAGE

WRITTEN BY
SHARON SWANEPOEL

God's Glory
Ministries International
Inc.

A GOD'S GLORY MEDIA PUBLICATION

Copyright © 2011 Sharon E. Swanepoel
All rights reserved under International Copyright Law. No part of this book may be reproduced or transmitted in any form or by any means, electronic or mechanical, including photocopying, recording, or by any information storage or retrieval system, without written permission of the author.

Author: Sharon Swanepoel
P. O. Box 1430, Dacula, GA 30019, USA.
www.GodsGlory.org
E-mail: sharon@godsglory.org

Illustrator: Lucas Loscinto
Website: http://strvnartist.googlepages.com/
E-mail: strvnartist@gmail.com. Tel: 540.710.4486

Layout and design: Rudi Swanepoel

The Adventures of Seek & Save: The Village
ISBN: 978-0-9772647-5-9

Thanks to:
My wonderful Heavenly Father for all Your love, mercy and grace. What a blessing to be part of the Great Commission. With my every breathe may Your glorious love be shown in declaring Your Gospel and making Your presence known. Living for You always.

My amazing husband Rudi. Every day together is a great adventure. You cannot begin to imagine how much your input, and that of the Holy Spirit, in my life has shaped me. Your belief in me is the thrust, to do what I never imaged possible. Thank you for your hours of work on the layout and design of this project. I love you.

Our God's Glory partners and ministry friends as well as family for your prayers and support.
Our God's Glory board of directors; Herb and Anita McDermott and Bill and Lynna Roberts, thank you for trusting in the vision God has given us and supporting us all the way. We love you.
Sam & Joyce Johnson and Priority One Missions, thank you for your encouragement and inspiring global mission outreach in our hearts. We are honored to stand with you for the Kingdom of God.
All who helped and participated in the Seek & Save Projects, especially Gene & Chris Brown. May the Lord richly bless you.
Joyce Squires, thank you for helping with the editing. You are a blessing to us.
Lucas Loscinto. Your illustrations rock!

A dedication to:
A true evangelist of the Gospel, Reinhard Bonnke. For all the many millions of lives changed by the Gospel message shared in Africa. The Adventures of Seek & Save was conceived in my heart by the Holy Spirit at the first Face to Face meeting in Orlando at CFAN.

CPSIA Section 103 (a) Compliant
www.beaconstar.com/ consumer
ID: K0111373. Tracking No.: L1312320-7820

Printed and bound in China

The African sun was rising in a golden glow
over the Mopani plateau.
Splat! Save swatted a huge mosquito,
while Seek was studying the map where to go.
Seek and Save were on a Safari in the Kalahari.

They had already spotted a big baboon and a dotted loon.
They gazed at the feast a lion was having on a big wildebeest.
This was Africa for sure. Here only the strong endure.
"Eat or be eaten," Save began to say,
And wondered who would be this lion's next prey.
"Let's move on," Seek said as they drove away,
still gazing upon the sight in dismay.
Suddenly they heard a loud crackle, "HEL-LO."
"HELLO," the sound came from below.
It was the voice of Tell on the CB Radio.
"Seek and Save, please come!" Tell cried.
"I have a new rescue mission for you."
"There is trouble in the Village of the Jumping Jabulani Tribe
and something is askew."
Save said, "Tell, we will leave here soon.
If we hurry we can be there by noon."

Tell was also in Africa visiting his friends
the Jumping Jabulani Tribe.
All was not well. He could feel a vibe.
Something he could not describe.
The Jumping Jabulani Tribe was a happy bunch
always dancing, singing, and well, jumping.
However when Tell entered the village this time
everybody was sad, sour and grumpy.

Even the milkshake they gave him to drink was bitter and lumpy.
His friend Chief Jabula seemed grumpy
and even looked a little frumpy!

Something was very wrong.
The Jabulani Tribe was silent and sang no welcome song.
Tell asked his friend, "Jabula what is wrong?"
He said, "Tell, my friend,
you have to help my village. Our jump is gone!"

Tell asked, "When did this all start?"
Jabula answered, "Since our water has turned bitter and dark.
Gummy the goat and Milky the village cow drank from the spring.
Then their milk turned sour.
Who could have thought such a thing?
The once clear water has turned bitter and black.
Tell, I think our village is under attack.
Everyone is sad and grim.
My patience is wearing thin.
Our jump is gone. This is very bad.
The lack of jumping is making me mad."
Tell said, "Just wait, Jabula, I know what to do!
My friends, Seek and Save, will help save the village and you!"

The sun was sitting high in the sky.
Seek and Save sat under a big tree
to have a 'Steak and Kidney' pie.
Save looked over the African plains and saw a giraffe.
Just then a pack of hyenas stared to laugh.
Their laugh was not a cheerful giggle like before,
Save could hear a note of pain at the core.
Seek saw zebras looking dusty, dirty, weak and thirsty.
All the animals they saw had their tongues hanging out.
What is this all about?

Seek said, "I have never seen such a sight!
Can this be the reason for Tell's invite?
How could these animals be thirsty with all this water around?"
"Yuck!" Echoing across the water came the alarming sound.
Way ahead on the water's edge they saw Thabo looking grim.
He had swallowed some of the water while taking a swim.

Thabo was Chief Jubula's son
and his swim had ended even before it had begun.
Seek asked, "Little boy, is there something wrong?"
"Well," Thabo started, "the water is bitter and". . .
"GONG, GONG, GONG" came the sound from the village below.
Then running towards the village,
Thabu cried out, "Lunch time. I have to go."

Up in the nearby tree Spunky Monkey was so thirsty
as he watched the scene below.
Moving his eyes side to side he watched the Jabulani Tribe
wallow in their sorrow.
Nobody knew the reason for the water being bitter and black.
They had no idea that Spunky Monkey was behind the attack.
Shaking his head he had to admit,
Spunky Monkey never liked the villagers one bit.
They were always jumping up and down.
He just could not take anymore.
Their jumping was very hard to ignore.

Actually, Spunky Monkey did not like anyone.
Not even his monkey family. He felt that he just did not belong.
He thought back to the day the bitter fruit had taken root.
The monkeys were sitting together in a group called a troop.
They were eating monkey 'fruity-de-toot-fruit' soup.
Spunky Monkey was always making trouble,
with the rest of the group.
He would tease Cooky Monkey, call her crazy,
and pull Punky Monkey's hair.
Then he would chase Chunky Monkey
and gaze at Blinky Monkey in a cross eyed stare.
He loved to show off his speed doing the loop de loop.
He swung through the trees letting out a loud "WHOOP!"

The animals and the villagers knew not to eat from the one tree
that stood alone on the African plain.
It was called The Trouble Tree by name.
It was said,
"Eating of this tree would lead to heartache and pain."

In the Trouble Tree Spunky could see
gleaming red fruit that seemed to call out, "EAT ME!"
Spunky Monkey climbed up and sat in the Trouble Tree.
Then he cried out loud, "So much fruit! All for me
as far as the eye can see!"
Then he ate not just one or two, but three.
The fruit was juicy and he shouted with glee, "YUMMY!"

Once he had eaten of it, he just could not stop.
He started to get a tummy ache
and it felt like his head would pop!
He remembered the warning but it was too late.
He had already made a grave mistake.

The half eaten fruit started to stink.
"Get rid of the evidence," he said to himself. "Where?
Think, Monkey think!"
So into the village water he threw the half eaten fruit.
"Let the Jabulani Tribe deal with it," he thought,
"but now it's time to scoot."

Spunky Monkey had no idea that his action
would poison the village water.
Or that he had been seen by the village chief's daughter.
Little Mbali played at the creek.
She was two years old and still could not speak.
But when she saw Spunky she let out a squeak.
Spunky pondered as he looked on the scene below.
"Did the sight of the Jabulani people being so thirsty
make him happy?" The answer was, "NO!"

While entering the village,
Seek and Save found Chief Jabula brushing the coat
of Gummy, his favorite goat.
They could see Chief Jabula was full of stress.
"What a mess."
"My friends, we have no Jabu Jabulani milkshakes
to welcome you with,"
Chief Jabula said grim.
The well known twinkle in his eye had grown dim.

Save noted that Milky Moo and Gummy Goat were looking weak.
The welfare of the tribe was looking bleak.
The entire village depended on Save, "the Brave"
and his brainy friend Seek, "the Geek."
Together they would find a solution,
even if they had to use a new technique.

Seek did some inquiry about what everybody had seen.
Thabo, who had swallowed some of the water,
was now looking green.
Bafana said he was the last one to drink
from the spring when it was sweet.
Now the water was bitter and smelled like stinky feet.

Only Mbali had seen what Spunky Monkey had done
so his secret was safe for now.
Somehow Tell knew that Seek and Save were able
to rescue this village and return milk to the cow.

Seek, Save and Tell slept around the camp fire that night.
Suddenly, they all awoke
to a shrieking sound with a dreadful fright.
Spunky Monkey had gotten thirsty
and went down to the water to drink.
The water in the darkness was as black as ink
with an awful stink.
Thirsty Spunky had slipped into the water and started to sink.
With ease Save pulled the soaking monkey from the water
faster than he could blink.

Alarmed at what just had happened
Spunky could hear his own heart pound.
Then he heard that annoying laughing sound,
giggling hyenas had gathered all around.

"They are laughing at me," he thought. His temper was short!
Leaping from Save's strong arms he landed in the nearby tree.
"Back to bed," Save said, "but first let's all have some Bush tea."
High up in the tree, above the three
drinking their tea, was Spunky.
He was thirsty, dripping wet, and very upset.
His visit to The Trouble Tree had only brought him regret.

Daybreak, the sun shone bright and it was very hot,
even if it was only six o'clock.
While looking at Milky Moo, Save said,
"Oh, what I would do for an ice cold Jabulani shake,"
and almost stepped on a snake that lay in the sun to bake.
"Be careful!" Tell said.
"Come have a slice of my famous granadilla cake."
While they were eating, Chief Jabula called a meeting.
He said, "There is no more drinking water," and so the entire
village stood beside the bitter water weeping.
Everybody in the Village was thirsty. They began to quarrel
and some of them began to fight.
This was not like the Jabulani Tribe.
It was a frightful and troubling sight.
The animals were cranky and had started to fight,
pushing and pulling with all their might.
Snapping at each other's tails, the crocodiles started to bite.

Seek and Save joined Tell at the village spring
and together they started to sing.
Over the dark water the song's cheerful notes began to ring.

SONG:
The solution to your problem is closer than you think.
Even when the problem you are facing starts to stink.
Know that when you ask God, you are standing at the brink
of the solution to the problem. You can find the missing link.

Any problem, God can fix it faster than you blink.
Problems great as mountains, to a mole's heap they will shrink.
Have faith in God, just trust Him,
for your doubt will make you sink.
He's the Solution to your problem. You'll be smiling in a wink.

The Jabulani Tribe gathered together to hear the song.
It did not take them long
to catch on, and so they all sang along.
The words brought courage and the tribe began to show
new hope as their faith began to grow.

Seek was examining the water in the spring.
"This is bad; I am not surprised the Chief is mad."
Seek said, "I have never ever seen such a thing."
"The cause of the problem has to be deep in the water,
so let's dive in."

"Save, are you ready to get wet?"
"Yes I am, Seek," came the reply. "Let's go for a dive! I am all set."
Tell waited at the water's edge.
"I will prepare a bite to eat for when you return," came his pledge.
So Seek and Save put on their flippers and goggles.
With their snorkels in place
they were ready to solve the village troubles.
Seek and Save dove in deep, waking the fish that lay asleep.
Still deeper they had to go.
DOWN, DOWN, DEEP and LOW, into the GLOOMY GLOW.

Seek saw it first and in disbelief he had to stare.
In the center of the spring was this disturbing sight
seeping out in front of them there.
It was a soggy, rotting, mush oozing, poisonous, bitter goo!
Seek moved in a little closer to inspect and decided what to do.
With a chubby finger pointed up, Seek showed Save to surface.
Wearing his dotted bathing suit,
Save looked like he belonged in a circus.

The entire Jabulani Tribe and Tell waited
for Seek and Save to come about.
Seek announced,
"There is an oozing fruit that has made the water bitter
and we must get it out!"
While thinking on what to do,
Seek paced back and forth,
his flippers flapping about.
It was quite a sight to see.
So Save gave a chuckle and poured Seek a cup of Red bush tea.
"Got it!" came the shout.

Seek, being ever prepared, kept a bag of salt in his tote.
"I have read that salt can make this kind of rotting fruit float,"
He said, and cleared his throat
then hummed a tune in a happy note.

He handed the bag of salt to Save, who threw it on the icky goo.
The rotting fruit started to float while the water turned blue.
Save knew just what to do to get rid of the goo,
it had an awful stink, "PHEW!"

He made a net and skimmed the gooey fruit
from the water's surface.
He then tossed the rotting fruit into the village furnace.
"That takes care of the rotting fruit." Save chuckled,
as he put on his boot and got his belt buckled.
Seek, still looked puzzled and said, "The water is salty instead!"
"We had great success in fixing the first part of this mess.
Now how do we fix the saltiness?"
"HMM?" Seek said while scratching his head.

Seek heard a buzzing sound. He looked all around --
then straight up, where he saw Spunky Monkey sitting in the tree.
Spunky got so nervous that he swung into the next tree
where he was painfully stung by a bee.
With a "YELP" Spunky leapt forward into Save's arms
letting out a whimpering plea. "EEE. . ."

"Now, now, let me see,"
Save said, removing the stinger.
He understood Spunky's plea as one that said: "HELP ME!"
Seek looked up and shouted out: "A hive, look there! See?"
"Where the bees are, there too the honey will be!"
Seek said, "I love honey, especially in my tea.
Honey will make the water sweet.
Every sip will be a treat."

Seek and Save, ever ready, had a plan.
Seek asked, "Save, could you chop that branch from the tree?"
Save answered, "Yes, I can."
"First we should find a new home for the bees."
"Ok," Save gave a patient sigh.
They placed the queen bee in another tree where the hive
could thrive.

The old hive was filled with honey
and Save closely looked at the tree.
It was a Healing Tree and it's leaves
could heal a cut on your knee.
In this tree even the fruit and flowers were sweet,
and the birds would greet with a happy tweet.

Save took an axe to the tree and the branch came down
with a loud 'CRACK' and a heavy 'THUD'.
Tell was so startled and almost slipped in the mud.
Finally there was a hefty 'SPLASH' as it hit the water.
They heard a shout of delight
as Mbali's father threw her up in the air,
and then again caught her.
Just then she started to speak. She said,
"Monkey throw fruit in water,"
loud enough for all to hear.
Spunky heard her loud and clear.
Then out of fear, his eyes started to tear.
He then fainted and fell from the tree,
smack in the middle of the tribe.
That's where he landed for all to see.

All at once the Jabulani Tribe closed in on Spunky
and one of them cried out, "Let's make monkey soup!"
A terrified Spunky came too,
as they were planning to make the stew.
The thought of himself in a soup
made him cry out in pain, "WHOOP!"
Spunky, once again jumped into Save's strong arms.
This time he did not let go.

Save said: "Tell, I think it's time
for you to share the Gospel story,
thinking of Spunky in a stew is just gory."
So Tell stepped forward and asked,
"Chief Jabula, can I tell the tribe of this great story I know?"
"Oh, yes, Tell, please do." Chief Jabula said, "We love good
stories. Let's hear it. On you go."

He then motioned for the tribe to sit down on the ground,
and they gathered all around.
Tell said: "This story is true,
and it speaks of the love God has for me and you.
It all began when God created man.
God named him Adam. He was made according to God's plan.
Adam loved being in the garden, but he was all alone.
So God made a woman out of Adam's rib bone.
They were very happy in Eden, the garden they called home.
Every day with God in the garden they would roam.

Just like The Trouble Tree, that has caused us such upheaval,
in Eden stood the tree called Knowledge, Good and Evil.
God said, "Adam of this tree you may not eat."
Adam heard and God did not need repeat.

One day the devil, as a snake, deceived Eve.
He told her to eat from the tree and more like God she would be.
That snake was oh, so discreet, in Eve's heart he placed deceit.
Adam and Eve both ate of the fruit.
Sin had taken root and so out of the garden they got the boot."

Chief Jabula said, "That's good! That's what we will do.
We will give Spunky Monkey the boot right into the soup."
Tell said, "Jabula, I am not done yet.
Dear little Spunky, do not fret.
I have yet another story for you.
Then you will see what you need to do."

Tell then told the tribe of the Bible story about Moses,
while Spunky planned to escape from right under their noses.
Tell told of the bitter water
that had the Israelites and Chief Moses in a daze.
It was a problem of pollution,
much like today in many ways.
Moses and God's people were in a bitter place.
Thankfully, God had a plan of grace.

For God told Moses to throw a branch
into the water and it became sweet.
The sweetness of God's love and provision cannot be beat.
Adam and Eve were the first people God ever made.
Because their mistake was grave, to sin we all became a slave.
So God had to find a way to pay, for man who had gone astray.
This price could only be paid by the shedding of blood.
This sacrifice was made to cover the greatness of sin's flood.

Because the first man sinned, we all do too.
Because of His love for us God had a plan to save me and you.
He made a way for us by sacrificing His Son, Jesus, on a cross.

Exodus 15:25
"So he cried out to the LORD, and the LORD showed him a tree.
When he cast it into the waters, the waters were made sweet."

The cross was made of wood,
so when we add the cross, to our lives,
it will remove the bad and add the good.
Jesus is the Branch that will make our hearts sweet.
His love will make our lives complete.
The Gospel (the good news of Jesus) is the solution
to sin's pollution.

Spunky, 'the village has been wronged by you,
but we all have sin in us too.'
If we confess, God forgives us for our sin
because of the price He paid.
We need to forgive as God has forgiven, today,
Chief Jabula, do not delay.
Sin is to blame for our hearts being full of bitterness,
shame and pain.
Like the village water, without Jesus our hearts taste the same.
Remember Jesus will make our lives sweet.
The sweetness of His love cannot be beat.
Just like Seek and Save cured the water
from being bitter and black,
so too, we need Jesus in our hearts to ward off sin's attack.
Jesus is the solution to sin's pollution.

Chief Jabula said, "Tell, what should we do?
I do not want our hearts to be bitter. Can Jesus change us too?"
Tell said, "Yes, Jabula, here is what you must do.
Pray this prayer and Jesus will save you."
The Village gathered together and all of them prayed the prayer.
In an instant Chief Jabula felt every care
be lifted off of him right there.

He started to Jump and the entire village joined him too.
"Our jump is back," he cried out while jumping about.
Spunky gazed in awe, his head askew.
Now he wondered, what will they do?
Celebrating, Seek and Save jumped for joy.
But Spunky was acting coy.

Chief Jabula now addressed Spunky,
who in turn acted very jumpy.
"Spunky you have been very bad.
You caused the entire village to suffer and this made me mad.
You knew not to eat of the fruit
and you deserve to get the boot.
However I realize we all make mistakes.
Being deceived we give in to the Devil's evil tempting snakes.
We forgive you, Spunky!" Chief Jabula said,
while he scratched Spunky behind his ears and patted his head.
Spunky was relieved and so happy that he jumped head over heels.
He then gave a cheerful "WHOOP! WHOOP!"
while doing cartwheels.

Spunky had been forgiven by the tribe and he felt so free.
It was true! Forgiveness held the key.
He would try to be nice to his monkey family,
and say he was sorry too.
He was not the same old Spunky Monkey, he felt brand new!
Even though the Jabulani Tribe wanted to put Spunky in a pot,
Spunky realized that he liked the Jubulani Tribe,
not just a little, but a lot.

Spunky was so glad that Seek and Save had come to the rescue.
He rejoiced that he had heard the Gospel message
that Tell knew.
So he joined the village in the Jabula dance,
so grateful that they had given him a second chance.
Seek and Save drove off into the sunset with their jeep,
happy this mission was complete.
For the Jabulani Tribe, the end to this story was very sweet.
Their jump was back and even higher than before.
Chief Jabula felt his heart would soar.
Their spring's water was sweet,
and they had a peace in their hearts that could not be beat.

This is the prayer the Jubulani Tribe prayed.
Their hearts now free and their fear swayed.
Knowing Jesus leads to a life that is blessed.
If you wonder: "Do I need Jesus?" The answer is, "YES!"
Let's pray together. You'll be changed forever.

Dear Jesus,
I ask you to come into my heart today.
Come and wash all my guilt and sin away.
Forgive me that in sin I went astray.
Make me your child, this I pray.
Lord, I forgive others like You have forgiven me.
So now in You I am free.
Teach me to walk in You, the Way.
All my cares and burdens on You I lay.
Thank you for loving me in every way.
Let me do Your will in all I do and say.
All this in Jesus Name I pray.
Amen.

Jesus said:
"The Son of man has come to seek and to save
that which was lost." Luke 19:10

MEMORY VERSES

Romans 5:8
But God demonstrates His own love toward us, in that while we were still sinners, Christ died for us.

John 7:38
He who believes in Me, as the Scripture has said, out of his heart will flow rivers of living water.

Ephesians 2:8
For by grace you have been saved through faith, and that not of yourselves; it is the gift of God

1 John 1:9
If we confess our sins, He is faithful and just to forgive us our sins and to cleanse us from all unrighteousness.

Luke 11:4
And forgive us our sins, For we also forgive everyone who is indebted to us. And do not lead us into temptation, but deliver us from the evil one.

Ephesians 1:7
In Him we have redemption through His blood, the forgiveness of sins, according to the riches of His grace.

JOIN SEEK & SAVE'S ADVENTURE

Get ready for the Mission to share the Great Commission.
This Mission Team makes the devil scream.
Help us rescue others as we trot the globe.
In sin they erode.
With God's act of love their sin will explode
and He will lift their heavy load.

How wonderful to share the greatest story ever told;
a message that will never grow cold.
Jesus still comes to seek and save the lost,
He paid the ultimate cost.

If you don't tell them they might never know.
This Good News you must show.
Do not stop at one, let the whole world know.
Then the Kingdom of God will grow.

Take on this mission and you will see,
part of Seek & Save's Gospel Adventure, you will be.
So do not wait.
With this book in hand you carry fresh Gospel bait.
Let your friends know about Jesus before it is too late.

QUIZ TIME WITH TELL

1. What was gone from the Jabulani Tribe?
2. What was the welcome drink of the Jabulani Tribe?
3. What made the rotting fruit float?
4. Who told Chief Jabula the Gospel story?
5. What did the Jabulani Tribe want to do with Spunky?
6. What was the fruit that Spunky Monkey ate?
7. Where were Seek & Save on Safari?
8. What must you do to be saved from your sin?
9. What is the name of the Village Tribe?
10. Who were biting their tails?
11. What did the hyenas do to make Spunky mad?
12. Why were the animals' tongues hanging out?
13. Who deceived Eve?
14. What did Chief Jabula do to Spunky?
15. What was the tree's name that God told Adam and Eve not to eat from?

Answers:

1. Their jump
2. Jabu Milkshakes
3. Salt
4. Tell
5. Make money soup
6. The Sinning Fruit
7. In the Kalahari
8. Confess and invite Jesus into your heart
9. The Jumping Jabulani Tribe
10. The crocodiles
11. They were laughing at him.
12. The water was bitter
13. The devil as a snake
14. He forgave him
15. Knowledge, Good and Evil

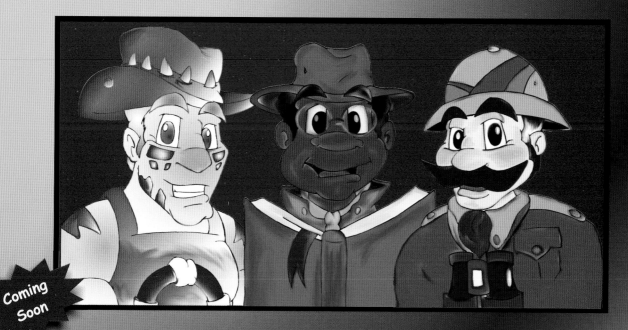

Coming Soon

Join Seek & Save on their next adventure.
This one takes them through the Amazon Rainforest
on their quest for:

The Temple of BLOOM

This new adventure
Coming Soon!

FIND US ON FACEBOOK

We're on Facebook
So, join us here and take a look.
Our work together is never done.
As we work, to share Jesus, God's own Son.
Together we have so much fun.
Sharing Jesus with everyone!

Seek and Save

Other Books in this series:

Lost at Sea

Lost at Sea
Audio CD & Songs
Order online at GodsGlory.org

Lost in the Dark

About the Author

Sharon has a great love for children and a heart for evangelism. She travels the world with her husband, Rudi, proclaiming the Gospel of Jesus Christ.

She is a friend of the next generation. Projects like this one is driven by her passion to encourage children to know Jesus, while teaching them the core truths that will equip them for life. Her vision is to place books like this in the hands of children worldwide and thus share with them the Good News of Jesus Christ early in their formative years.

An accomplished musician / composer with several published Cd's, she has entered into a this genre with a prayer for transformed lives all over the world.

For more information visit www.GodsGlory.org

Sharon Swanepoel

Lucas Loscinto

About the Illustrator

Lucas is an artist with a tremendous God-given ability to bring characters to life. He has a heart for children, and passion for God.

Email: strvnartist@gmail.com